MW00680831

I Have His Letters Still

Poetry of Everyday Life

by

Ray Brown

INFINITY
PUBLISHING

ISBN 0-7414-6074-2

Printed in the United States of America

Published August 2010

INFINITY PUBLISHING
1094 New DeHaven Street, Suite 100
West Conshohocken, PA 19428-2713
Toll-free (877) BUY BOOK
Local Phone (610) 941-9999
Fax (610) 941-9959
Info@buybooksontheweb.com
www.buybooksontheweb.com

Dedications

To my wife, Susan
whose love and encouragement and proofreading
made this all possible

To my now, eleven children,
Anthony, Chrissy, Michael, Teresa, Fernando, Marisa, Angela,
Dominic, Grant, Reid, Jillian
who give life meaning and in turn meaning to my poems

To Isabella and Gabriella
looking forward to the day they can read their grandfather's work
and write poetry with him

To Warren Cooper, Carol Muzychko, and
Elijah B. Pringle, III
my proofreaders and the best of friends.
Warren and Elijah are fellow poets

To Ginny Bournias and Lois Hess
who were always there

To Bruno Tarzia
a Bayonne, New Jersey poet who offered to take a new poet under
wing and provided a mystique for my
creative works

To Jake
an 8th Grade Student from California who got stuck with writing a
report on a poet,
and was glad to discover I was alive

Contents

II

III

v

Index

The Poetry Club
35 East 39th Street
Bayonne, NJ 07002

11-9-89

Dear Ray,

The poetry chart is sent under separate cover along with this, which is being written this a.m. (5:30!) — to give an example of my varying sleeping hours lately. An impromptu envelope for the chart was rigged from a larger last night and prepared last night for early mailing, but I thought something should be said that it was put together at a time when information on each "form" was available by hunting up separate volumes on versification not easily available. The Japanese "haiku" then was known (slighter) by the term used in the chart "hokku". The dictionary carries both terms now. I think the Second World War poets who went to the Pacific, or writers who visited Japan later, were responsible for the change — to break from "tradition".

The chart has been praised by two Pulitzer Prize Poets and used in NY University of Adults Study Catalog as a useful aid, and the South Carolina College for Women (Winthrop College) adopted it for several years. I do have numerous authorities who praised it highly.

Anyway, if you need help later on, let me know.

Bruno

PS — Avoided using the typewriter because of the early hours and there's a baby downstairs from me.

"I Learned to Kill for You" – *page 3*

(by Teresa Alessandria De Sapio of TADS-Art & Illustration)

I

I Learned to Kill for You

≈

Just 19, I was ferried through the desert
in a copter. We worried that the eternal sands
of this enemy's land would choke the intakes.

I had prepared for this,
sharpened my shooting eye,
learned to clean, assemble and disassemble,
mastered the correct hold
to choke the air intake of the enemy, to bring death.

Honed my physique,
fine tuned my body to pain,
practiced war games on the video screens,
bonded with these comrades
with whom I would shortly alight.

Now as we step onto the battle field
I am taken aback by the immediacy
of the enemy's onslaught.
I had worried about how it would feel
the first time -

But found there was no time to feel – or think.
Instinct and reflex governed.

I simply killed for you.

A Stepping Stone Job

≈

A stepping stone job.

He crossed the big pond
in the wheel well of a Boeing 767
in search of a stepping stone job.

An accountant who lived in a country without any money.
"To move from your own country,"
his mother lamented – "why?"

Cold — damp — dark —
they sold him a portable oxygen tank and mask —
the kind his father used
        -- before his death.

A forged Aeroflot maintenance ID card
to reach the tarmac at JFK –
whisked away in the waiting van
to manage fellow иммигрант émigré travelers
as Street Walkers in Jamaica Queens
in his stepping stone job.

A Poet's Dream

≈

It's times like this
    the beach would be a good companion.
Just the waves, the wind, and seclusion.

I'd write then for the water,
    talk to gulls to persuade them of my friendship.

Perhaps some greatness would come of it.
For in my heart,
    I feel some simple message which asks only
       for the time, the sand, the beach, and a pen.....
To find life.

The Mask of Many Faces

≈

There once was an ordinary man
who masqueraded as a clown.
Upon his sleeve, he wore but false emotion.

His countenance bespoke everything - and nothing.
Perpetual sadness ensconced within,
his face slipped on the mask of the occasion,
the personage for whom designed,
or of the time, perhaps –
or of the moment, so inclined.

So often having changed expression
he stood now perpetually expressionless.
The face his own, or a mask?
No one, not even he, could tell.

An endless fluidity of persona, ebb and flow.
Harmonized not with appearance.
Deceived as much by appearance -
as appearance deceived.

White the cosmetic through which he sought unveiling.
Unburden for once and for all
the role he played
for which the world accepted him.

White cream produced white heat instead
though no amount of flame could shear the crust which overlay –
Rawhide replace where once stood beauty,
Tenderness of touch,
Warmth of smile.

Invention upon invention!
Fiction now ruled
and sophistry imprisoned him.
A sorcerer's fate for a simple man.

Now no more a child's idol –
employed at Mardi Gras.
Grotesque false face of carnival.
Perjured soul.
Splendid thing – now lost.

Can fable save some touch of mediocrity
to mark the bounds of true complexion?
Perchance the tears of time
will wash away
what otherwise cannot be moved.

≈

I Once Believed It All

≈

I once believed it all.

The tales of valor
now strewn on the battle fields of reality.

The spirit of hope
dashed upon the rocks of disappointment.

The expectation of love
lost so quickly in the thicket of emotion.

The fulfillment of faith
evaporated in the disbelief of misplaced trust.

Heroes unmasked.

Yet was it they who led me to this point,
or did I craft the mask?

Her Fingerprints upon His Heart

≈

Not so hard a man
he found his touch against her cheek
enough of a message of tenderness
to warm him.

They would walk
along the tow path of the canal
by the placid Delaware River
near Stockton NJ.

They talked of life
of why, and here, and now,
and understanding.

In a walk once through Tinicum Park,
on the Pennsylvania side, while holding hands
they stopped and turned towards one another
and as the near silent breeze
rustled the leaves of fall, they kissed -
an imprint of emotion.
There was within both, this urge of passion
but somehow it was tenderness
that drew them together.

They enjoyed the shad fest at Lambertville
feed each other by hand
little portions of warm sustenance
and then again, the Chamber concert
at the Lutheran Church in Erwinna.

One day – as fall turned to winter - she was gone...

She left alone, her fingerprints upon his heart.

Unemployed

≈

I knew this would be a tough morning for him
just having lost his job at age 52
his wife, three young children,
a mortgage like an albatross around their necks,
a car loan, ballet lessons, soccer camp,
and the looming $100,000 bill for college.

Who could take this all?

I knocked on his door around 10 am,
a time he would not usually be at home.
Actually rang the doorbell.
I had a box of those round doughnut holes
and a little carrier of Morning Joe.
He had on a bathrobe, partially opened
that looked like it hadn't been worn since he was in college
a one day old scraggly beard.
If he were Marlon Brando or Broderick Crawford
I'd expect him to have a cigarette dangling from his lips.

The house was immaculate, his wife kept it that way
got the kids off to school, and then left each morning
for her job at the County library in the research department
answering lately e-mails from people
who wanted to know
the latest economic and employment forecasts

but most of whom asked whether there was an on-line source
they hadn't already checked to find a job.

What could you say
to this once proud man -
not a man of extraordinary ego
just a man who worked hard to make a living
loved his family, took only a little piece of the American dream,
the one that hard work bought.

To be without a job
ready, willing and able to contribute
to receive that severance notice
is like a pin prick to an inflated helium balloon
the air exhausts quickly
the balloon shrivels to a small crumpled remnant of its former self,
falls to the earth.
You can't put the air back into something
that is no longer whole.

Gradually I eased him into talking.

At first it didn't work
but within a half an hour
he was dropping those little doughnut holes
into his coffee mug and jamming them with a spoon
breaking them apart, gobbling the mess between words.

→

Unemployed – 3

≈

I eased out of him his severance package of a couple of
months
how for at least that time his financial life could be the
same.
I asked him if his wife had changed in but these 24 hours.
Or if his children had even noticed -
I suggested he not give them something to notice.

I told him about the unemployment office,

where it was located, and how not to let disgrace
be his companion when he walked there,
about the group of us who now had a table
in the local library where we checked the Internet
swapped stories about job visits
read each other's resumes.

At about 10 am we'd visit the local Dunkin' Donuts
a cup of coffee still in our respective budgets.
I'd left them there this morning to visit this friend
whom I now invited to become a part
of our newly established fraternity.

It had been four months. I was finally off of Zoloft.
Only took Lunesta on rare occasion.
He recognized me now, no longer a vacant stare.
Remembered his visit to me six months earlier.
Then he came at 7:30 am -- he had a job.

I appreciated the visit

but he never quite understood,
hadn't discovered yet, how much it takes out of you
leaves you vacant,
dispirited,
feeling worthless in a world that measures
value by dollars and cents.

I know not what the future brings
but know there is a future
will walk this path because I see it well-worn by others.
We will make it, we will all make it.
And then I am not sure what Dunkin' Donuts will do.
When we had jobs, we used to visit Starbucks.

≈

At the End of the Day

≈

At the end of the day...

The worries of the next arise from their daytime germination.

Content in the parched earth,
    having awaited their opportunity,
    now entwined in the synapses
    until, like weeds in a garden
    they choke out the rich hues of the evening
    sunset
shadowing the golden yellow flowers.

At the end of the day...

One last chance to pull the sprouts emerging from the seeds
of doubt
    before their tentacles root,
    choking out the dainty fingers of the flowers
    which held on during the long day.
The beating noontime sun having sapped their strength,
    now breathe a sigh, wearied...
    reaching the oasis of evening.

At the end of the day...

The weeds bundled and tied.
He splashed some tepid water from the barrel on his face
        and then trod wearily through the door of inner self,
        seeking solace in his bed -- and comfort for his mind.
While in the garden his next day worries sprouted once
again,

At the end of the day...

≈

Birthday Wishes

≈

The 55 candles on his cake burned brightly.

Family gathered round,
there was now one grandchild,
a new addition on this birthday.

He had gone through a number of trials,
yes travails, to reach this point.
There were times when he did not think
he would make it.
Just too much to do
and not enough to do it with.

Not enough time.
Not enough money.
Not enough energy.

His wife and children encouraged him
to make a wish -
"Make a wish and blow."

"But I don't have anything to wish for," he said.
"Everything is just perfect.
I have everything I need."

"Then wish that nothing will change," his wife said.

"Just wish – that nothing will change…"

Black Cat

≈

A black cat crosses no path by coincidence.
It searches for its prey, as meticulously
as the lion tracks the wildebeest, circles
then runs it down.

The gatto nero understands its role.
Select one each day - for whom
normal misfortune is insufficient.
Then predict, for no predictable cause,
a tragedy indelibly etched on the mind
by the vision of the cat,
in the pathway of life.

Why stalk its victims? "Why not", it answers.
This widely held secret –
it succeeds less than 25% of the time.
Batting average is .249.

The coincidence of circumstances - not whom the cat
chooses,
but whether it has chosen someone
whom fate elects to notice that day.

As for the cat, its reputation precedes it.
Little does the world note its failings.
People consider themselves lucky
to have avoided the divination -
to talk about it further would be bad karma.

I Have His Letters Still

≈

When I was young
they were kept in a shoebox.
Then, in late middle age,
in an old leather correspondence case,
found at a flea market,
kept in the bottom desk drawer.

Handwritten in flowing cursive script
by original Lewis Waterman pen
point dipped in a well
the fountain of personal essence
the blue flowed with emotion
like the waters of life.

Soul captured not by Lucifer
but by the fiber of the paper
crafted in Egypt along the Nile
history nested so deeply between the reeds
weaved invisibly
between the threads of papyrus.

The envelope, self-sealed in a meticulous way
with wax, monogrammed
engraved so beautifully on the back.
The Steamboat Savannah stamp
hand canceled – May 24, 1944
a distinctive ink which marked its journey
as would a traveler his journal
from South Carolina to Baptistown, NJ.

I treasure this letter, and its envelope.
When I pick it up and read
I feel him rising
through the warmth of his words,
grasping my hand...
this post saved in the attic of my memories.

While I have other poets today
their presence I see just fleetingly
on the computer screen,
my palm touch against the monitor
only makes work for me
with Windex.

Though a friend taught me about the "Save" button
I feel as if I have saved nothing, and lost much
each time I push/click -
their correspondence lost –
in impersonal set aside.

Why time took this treasured means of human discourse
there is no answer.
Does it have no sense of history -
permanency?
Upon my death, for what
will they use my leather satchel?

Thankfully -- I have his letters still.

≈

"The Lady with Bumps on Her Head" – page 22

II

The Lady with Bumps on Her Head

≈

Rome, Italy

Campo de' Fiori was bustling
in the bright springtime sun
maneuvering through the tent booths
of the Italian farm market
this Medieval fair
provides color and excitement—
fresh fruit, nuts,
and a festive bright pink "Ciao Bella" t-shirt
for my Italian-Mexican-American granddaughter.

Here I found
Newark Airport's shoeshine stand's international twin
seated on a rickety fruit box
with a plywood board
and a shining rag which had seen better days.
His four year old daughter picking through something
on the pavement next to him.

I brought packages of Italian tomato seeds
for my 90 year old father at home
then passed a lady in black,
whose face I would not see
squatted in the foot path between two stalls
swaying—now undulating—back and forth
staring at the pavement
the top of her head exposed
her wrinkled palm open—
a human collection plate propped up by her knee.

In 1966 in New York, my mother had taught me
about "beggars" in the streets.
Most unemployed men .
Appearances deceived, she taught,
while they appeared "down on their luck"
it was drink, not luck,
that defined their station.

So at age 17 in Manhattan,
cock sure that the world's ills were there for me to fix,
I told him I would not give him a quarter
but would go to the Automat with him
buy him the cup of coffee
for which he begged a contribution.
He proved my mother's point.

This elderly Italian lady though
could not be faking the seven round hematomas on her
skull.
I did not see her face
a face of sorrow she did not care to share
or did not know she could.

As I reached into my pocket for some Euro coins
whose value I did not yet appreciate.
I was sure my mother would have understood.

≈

The Measure of a Man

≈

As they sat in the hard oak pews
at their brother's funeral
they heard the minister ask:
"What is the measure of a man"?
and while this pastor who gave the eulogy
barely knew their brother
they internalized their grief
and remembered now, long ago days,
though not care free, they seemed that way.

The days along the riverside,
where they dug with their hands for worms,
fished together,
then, when they were sure no one was watching
or no longer cared
dipped their naked bodies into the cool water.
Ran home later - the three Amigos
with dry clothes so not to add
to their mother's burden -
to make sure -
they would get their early afternoon chores completed
so when their father returned from the tannery at night
they could await his judgment -
What measure would he take of them, as his sons?
-        soon to be men.

Thereafter they each struggled with their education
then to find a job in their home town
before there were true options to look beyond
how they would work two, sometimes three jobs,
then guide their own children through a different world -
one somewhat unfamiliar, even intimidating to them -
a world of words and choices,
much different than the times of their youth.

They struggled, worked hard
laughed long when their three families
shared their communality
at times of joy and sadness.

Now with his death, their brother's name
will not be written permanently anywhere -
except upon his headstone.
No great enduring singular deed
no discovery, no wide adulation,
the author of his obituary
does not wax poetic
about the course of the world's orbit
deprived of his thoughts.
His deeds and his life's measure
lie but for a short time
in his footprints in the sand,
soon worn away by the tides of time....

→

The Measure of a Man – 3

except perhaps what mark his children might yet make.

His two brothers understood this.
This wisdom a rare gift.

And so, when at the cemetery, the two
took their own measure,
by laying on the green grass atop their purchased plots
to determine whether when their time came
they would fit within their tombs
there were but few of the mourners,
those outside of the family,
including the pastor who gave the eulogy,
who misunderstand the exercise.

≈

Mums

I remember the yellow mums
that adorned the mothers' sweaters
in those autumn days of the early 60s
when football games were played in the sunlight
on a Saturday afternoon.
Times were more casual,
although the games just as intense.

Then they were known as
the Delaware Valley Regional High School Terriers.
40 years later, Terriers are not
an aggressive enough mascot --
so now they call themselves "the dogs".

Then, mums told all there was to say
about a mother's pride
a sense of loyalty to the hometown
how beauty was displayed in simplicity,
and wearing flowers at a football game
was still touching.

They were all there, in the bleachers,
the day when Rick Long had his concussion.
He got kicked in the head
tackling the fullback
for South Hunterdon Regional High School
on Thanksgiving Day.

≈

Mums - 2

The mothers gasped,
as he lay so motionless on the field.
Then applauded
as he walked off in a daze
to wander the sidelines.

The whole group consoled Mrs. Long
the sorority of strong women
there for their children,
not because they particularly liked football.

The next morning, a floral arrangement
arrived at Fran Long's home
just in time for Thanksgiving dinner.
This one had the yellow and blue school colors,
but also had the deep crimson and white
the pinks and oranges,
and the little yellow popcorn mums
to fill in between.

Fran was touched by this all.....

and now – 40 years after Rick's passing
she tends her bed of mums
on the hillside near her driveway entrance.
She has not been back to a football game since.
Today new lights from the field,
blaze and announce the Friday night games -
she lives close enough to hear the crowd roar

after each good tackle,
as they first cheered, then grew eerily silent
after Rick's.

She knows some young high school girls
undoubtedly still wear the mums
since she finds her yellows,
missing from the hillside garden on Saturday mornings,
plucked at the base
by high school boys
who stop quickly after school
and furtively snips a stem or two
on the afternoon before the Friday night game.

When she notices, she is not upset.
She smiles but a wry little smile.
Ricky, she images, would have done the same -
stopped quickly at someone's Mum garden
clipped a few without asking -
as he was driving past
in his 66 Chevy Impala
on the day before the '67 Thanksgiving game.

≈

A Still Small Voice

≈

The artist's melody infused the room.
Embraced the audience.
A violin, a cello, a flute,
a fine tuned piano.

I held her hand
spoke to her in a still, small voice.
Like a bow to the strings of a violin,
        it resonated.

Quiet words fashioned -- whiffed softly through the night air
tenderly touch the soul
warm the heart.

As we left the chamber hall
I kept this instrument -
a subtle timbre now stirs finer words
no assertive boisterous clamor,
grandiose gesture or performance.
No cymbals or drums.
A subtle melody of human understanding.

I am glad I found this still, small voice.

Talking in Bed

≈

Vacations are perfect for laying
and talking in bed.
Relationship reinvigoration.

Back home
beds are for sleeping
or making love when we are not too tired.

Back home
beds are for guilt trips in the morning.
We would not be caught in the morning in bed
just laying and talking.

Back home,
if we got caught talking in bed in the morning
I would make an alibi -
that we were merely making love, merely having sex.

Love in the morning is
what you call laying in bed, just talking,
when you are on vacation.

The Cliff on Which You Stand

≈

Twice I called out to you
and twice my words reverberated against
the concrete walls
that held you firm upon the hillside.

With no handholds carved within that foundation
no fissure within the cliff face
I cannot even crawl to your feet.

You stand so tall against the horizon
you will see me I am sure
if you care to glance down.

Laying in Wait

≈

There is a plant that lies in wait for flies.
Curious plant – whose whole existence underset on trapping someone.

It lives and breathes and grows.
But could not do so, would not be happy, without the lure and the receptacle.

There are people like that.
They live and breathe and eat - and lie in wait.
Use each stratagem or device to betray and trick,
expose those who are kind enough to be their victims.

Yet unlike the flytrap, they do not grow.
And unlike Venus, they do not love.
But like us all, they live and die.
Be wary – lest you consume yourself.

This was our time to be children

≈

We foraged through the garbage dumps
scrounging for food to embellish our emaciated forms,
in adolescent years
searching for the objects which could produce
some small sum for our families.

We did this - not knowing,
        this was our time to be children.

Planes....
we could hear the whirring of the bombs
then the implosion
as they decimated the landscape
leveled our villages
took and covered our parents -
as the fires of the napalm seared our skin.
We cried the wail of orphans
and sang the songs of those
too young to understand.

We did this - not knowing,
        this was our time to be children.

We marched, shackled at first at the ankles
then released to march again
a Kalashnikov AK – 47 strapped on our backs
a new pair of combat boots,
we murdered women, children,
our ancestors, our countrymen,
this was our education
this our mission.

We did this – not knowing,
           this was our time to be children.

Grabbed from the bosoms of our mothers
sold and carried off
carted across the sea
housekeeping in the shadows on Park Avenue
locked in small rooms
adjacent to the pantries we cleaned.

We were sold to service those whose deranged minds
sought consolation in power over the powerless -
we watched our replacements come at age 9.

This was our lot – not knowing,
           this was our time to be children.

They wrapped our feet when we were four
and did not remove the Golden Lotus binding,
on crippled toes, carried burdens like pack animals.

Across another continent without anesthesia,
elders took pieces of broken glass
snipped our clitoris
stitches of thorns used to control our bleeding.

Our fathers came into our beds
their weight atop us paled
the weight atop our minds.
We carried these rocks like the stone of our countenance.
                    →

This was out time to be children – 3

when they did these things

We did not know – this was our time to be children.

When you heard you cried for us –
        by then, we no longer knew of tears -

You told us that if you knew
you would have wrapped us
swaddled us in a warm blanket
like the one in your layette
comforted us, brushed our hair
told us fairy tales, taken us to the zoo
let us pet the lambs at the farmer's fair
swim in a crystal blue pool
dive from the board

listen to music, and dance...
kick a soccer ball
these were the things, you said,
that children did -

except - there was no longer time for those things

the time to be children had passed
along with our innocence.

When all this transpired – we did not know

              it was our time to be children.

36 | P a g e

Going Down

≈

.....Mark 4:35-41

Hey Lord.
Don't you care, that we are going down?
....sucked into the vortex of unknown fear
the swirling black hole
which pulls at our every fiber.
Where are you,
when I really need you?
I am just a few steps ahead of the quicksand.

It seems as if you sleep
uncaring
and even when I call -
do not awake.

I do not care that the wind and the sea
may listen to you eventually.
I need you now.
Now is when I am terrified,
do not understand,
when I fear I will break apart.
I've seen you cut others loose
known them to go down with the ship.
Is that my fate?

If you intend to save me,
Why put me through this peril to begin with?

Birds on Furlough

A patriotic resident of New Jersey
I put my birds on furlough.

No tinkle of bird seed in the feeders on Fridays this year.

The first week they appeared on my window sill
no warm morning songs of greeting
questioning little expressions.
They had heard about these cutbacks
from their friends in other communities
their vacant eyes incredulous
if they could verbalize, would say **"Et tu, Brute?"**.

I listened to all the talking heads on TV
stood my ground
not wanting to show any sign of weakness --
but I was haunted by their eyes.

Within two weeks they staged a protest
the string purloined from Home Depot
little pieces of protest signs
left on the Capitol steps by CWA and NJEA members
they weaved their placards of indignation
and festooned my trees to greet me early one morning.

By this point, I had had it.
The morning sunlight of the spring,
invigorated air filled with the scent of lilacs
wafted through the sliding glass door.
I pushed the screen door aside
stood firm upon the patio steps
and yelled "**you're all lucky to have jobs**".

The birds have flown the coop so to speak,
tightened their belts,
found their morning nourishment
in the farm fields of nature
spying my world from contiguous trees.

Bird feeders silent
like the great engines of American's factories
like the orchestras of small towns
silenced by the donors.

My mornings are lifeless now
stuck with a cup of black coffee
a dried English muffin, no Star-Ledger
no songbird morning joy to nourish me
now -- only memories in the backyard of my mind

this, since I did my patriotic duty
        and put my birds on furlough.

≈

A Day Aptly Named, Black Friday

≈

She was crushed to death on Black Friday.
First in line at the local Wal-Mart
she arrived at 2 am.
The crowd filled in behind her
got more antsy as the hours passed,
the temperature started to dip,
on a day approaching winter
more than Indian Summer.

Though the store was scheduled to open early at 5:30 am
people started to push around 4:30.
At first just irritating -
then disconcerting -
finally the jostling morphed into jousting,
became a real concern.

Disoriented she tried to hold her ground
the back of her thighs ached, tightened
from being pushed to the tips of her toes
like a ballerina, which she wasn't.
A rope divider in front of her
like the red carpet at the Oscars
cordoning off the line
to leave enough space so the store
could actually open the doors when the hour came.

About 4:55
pushed up a few inches at a time
she tried to yell for people to ease off

no one could hear -
except for the few in the same predicament directly behind her -
the deafness of impending catastrophe.

The crowd acting as if in Times Square at New Year's,
started a countdown to the opening hour.
By 5:25 no more than a few inches from the glass
she started to rap, with her purse.
She had no idea that her own death was imminent
it was not in the sales flyer -
although not prone,
fear spread through her veins
as if she lay flat over the pit with the pendulum's blade
moving closer and closer to her chest.

When the blue coated attendants appeared
on the other side of the plate glass
the crowd surged.
Slapped against the pane
the way she had once slapped a rude patron in a bar,
crushed against the door
as if in a giant human vice,
she attempted one last futile call
just before she lost all breath.
Diaphragm and lungs flatted like a pancake.

→

A Day Aptly Named, Black Friday – 3

≈

Few of her Wal-Mart "shopping colleagues"
ever noticed her predicament
too busy reading the sales signs
or the coupons they held in their hands like prayer cards.

When they straightened out the hysteria,
- a story in and of itself -
her lifeless body slumped to the sidewalk.

Sobbing, crying, screaming hysterically
a 17 year old high school senior
working part time
saw the whole thing from the lobby of the store
inches away, separated from death by plate glass
watching Black Death's work
as one would watch Piranha in an aquarium
eat the others.
Observed life's form, as it left the shopper,
fog the outside of the door pane glass.

Later she would be haunted by the likeness
left in last breath's steam on the panel
like's Christ's face on Veronica's veil
this poor soul, human sacrifice to a strange god
which required attendance at the Churches of Commerce
on the Friday after Thanksgiving.

What was bred from us
that this crowd could continue on its way
walk right over the body
as they would walk past a homeless man
curled in a sleeping blanket on the street
on the sidewalk in New York?

To be only 17
stand helpless
in the face of another's death.

Who can comprehend
why this should be -
why it came to pass -
crushed to death by her own people
on a day aptly named - Black Friday.

≈

"Santa Sanctorum" – page 68

III

I Have Never Been A Soldier

≈

I have never been a soldier except in my childhood games.
I have never pushed my physical endurance to the edge.
Only theorized about the forces of good and evil,
　　　never confronted them face to face.
Never looked death in the eye
　　　to determine whether I would blink.
Never had to ask myself whether I could pull the trigger,
　　　to take a life.

Never had to test my metal in the face of the enemy.
Decide whether I could lay my body upon a grenade
　　　so others might live,
　　　　　discover whether I could subordinate
　　　　　myself to the good of all.

Never,

　　　- after having endured all this,
　　　- killed for the greater good,
　　　- saw friends expire in my arms,
　　　- watched my duty commingle with evil
　　　and worry whether I could tell the difference....

Never left to wonder,
about the essence of my being,
whether it all made any sense.

These things were never in my childhood imagination.
Battles were always won.

I never came home to a sleepless night.

Never dreamed myself in a cockroach infested
        VA Hospital.
Never walked the streets
        looking for a quarter for a cup of coffee.
Never envisioned a marriage
        that would not survive the nightmares.
Never in my synapses
        felt the presence of an arm that was not there.
Never felt ostracized by those
        who lived back home in comfort and safety
        when all I did was perform my duty
as well as any common man when put to the test.

Humbled now by those who lived these things.
In awe of what they have endured.
I salute their valor –

ashamed that all I have, are the war games of my mind.

≈

I'm Tired

≈

I'm getting tired now.
My eyes are heavy.
My hand is slow.
Even my pen loses patience with me.

People have wearied of coaxing me to sleep.
They're afraid I will not arise.
Would you want responsibility for persuading
        one to rest when you knew they would not awake?

So let me go –
Let me be...
Let my pen be the one who runs out of ink.
Not me.

On the Other Side of the Bi-Fold Screen

≈

James called from behind the screen.
A distinctive definitive voice,
querulous about his station,
intending to come out on his own time
but uncertain nonetheless.
Knowing that I was there, awaiting him,
would make it easier for him to disclose himself.

I heard him call again, I did not answer -
he did not come -
the screen was folded, he was not there -
only my reflection in the mirror on the wall
on the other side of the bi-fold screen.

What Progress Has Wrought

≈

A friend of mine, an anthropologist,
lived in the Australian outback
with an aboriginal tribe for 30 months.
He returned to New Jersey.
One sunny October day
driving along the Delaware River
on Route 29, from Stockton to Frenchtown,
the palisades which claimed the river as their own
looming above on both sides,
he approached the Devil's Tea Table
a flat, plateau rock outcropping
180 feet above the travelled way
protected by hordes of brown and tan
poisonous, copperhead snakes.

There below Satan's table
on the shoulder of the roadway
he beat the State of New Jersey
Department of Transportation
contracted Deer Carcass removal company
when he stopped and picked up the body of a deer
which had lost an argument with another vehicle.

At home, in the farm field
he gutted and skinned the buck
hung the meat to dry
and from the hide fashioned some leggings,
sewed for himself a pair of winter snow boots.

The ribs he would carve into his New Jersey
version of an amulet, the rack of antlers
he ground into an aphrodisiac powder,
most of the entrails
he would bury in his garden plot
to decompose as fertilizer.
Whatever litter he left in the field
the scavengers made good use of.

No part unattended
no stone unturned.

When the New Jersey DEP, Division of Fish
Game and Wildlife
learned of his rebellious act, they fined him $ 750
in the Kingwood Township Municipal Court
for procuring wildlife, although dead,
without a permit.
It made no difference that he saved them $ 75 -
the cost the State paid the contractor
to remove each carcass, then
haul the remains to the incinerator in Warren County
where it would add to all our troubles,
its emissions needing scrubbing
before the crisp blackened deer smoke could pollute the air.

→

What Progress Has Wrought – 3

≈

While he had been awarded a full professorship
at Princeton
he packed that night, used the satchel he
had tanned from the balance of the pelt
which they did not notice
when they confiscated the boots and carvings
as the ill gotten gains from his illegal activity
all stored by the State in a warehouse in Trenton
along side the unlicensed shotguns
and racks of antlers from poachers
who hunted with their headlights in the evening.

What remained of the entrails not yet decomposed
together with a portion of the dirt from his garden
he boxed up and posted for
overnight delivery to the Commissioner of DEP,

and thereafter, he left quietly that same night
and returned to Australia.

≈

Ship of State

≈

My ship of state
still afloat after 60 years.
Tossed again today by stormy seas.

I refuse a GPS as a matter of principle.
I watch for lighthouses...
Now watch them disappear.
Needless incidents of history.
How quickly they forget those who guide us.

A wooden hull,
marred and marked by my encounters with the shoals -
the rocks of life against which I throw it.
The hidden sand bars no less daunting.
Now I sail in defiance.
My regrets tossed overboard
with the other damaged goods.

In middle life they tried to steer me
towards a new craft.
A shiny plastic one
designed for seamless repairs.
But I liked the wood
and the inefficient time I spent in sanding,
reflecting where it had been
what it had endured
and where we yet would go.

→

Ship of State - 2

≈

For years the crews have come and gone.
Earlier shanghaied,
I and they having no choice.
Now I pass the mighty vessels of their lives.
They - thankful for the training.
I – thankful for their gifts.

Today a skeleton crew,
of family and a few close friends.
There for curiosity, companionship,
and to watch an old man.

They perform essentially a maintenance function –
for both ship and captain.
Searching not to change or grow
but to hold steady the course
until that one last storm.

Afterwards they will remark:

> **"She was a fine ship
> and he
> an able Captain."**

≈

Shoveling Snow on Wii

≈

School is closed, my son is bored.
I have just come in from shoveling snow -
The driveway, the sidewalk.
The walk of the elderly lady next door,
        who is housebound.

He is in his bedroom with the door shut,
arguing and yelling at his younger brother.

When I was thirteen
I had a paper route each morning before school.
Walked or rode my bike
threw the papers toward each porch.
Took pride in perfecting my throw
to where I was accurate to a pinpoint eighth of an inch.
Eventually built a stamina,
threw effortlessly and efficiently --
to avoid tipping over the milkman's bottle.

On days of snowstorms
I'd run up to the porch,
hand the papers to a sleepy audience,
hope I'd be asked
if school had been cancelled
        and if I had time to shovel the walk.

→

Shoveling Snow on Wii - 2

≈

The route done, I ran home,
grabbed the shovel I had purchased
        with my own snow shoveling earnings
and spent the morning shoveling walks –
and the porch of the house bound lady next door for free.

In the warmth of my inner hallway
I shook the snow off my daydream
opened the bedroom door.
My son has the Wii Remote Classic Controller
in his hands.

On the screen are two figures -
the Mii avatars of my boys
each little twit shoveling furiously,
piling scoop upon scoop of snow on the heap
as the weight meter chronicled their efforts.

Since when do they have snow shoveling on Wii?

≈

Airline Pilot, Hero of Flight 1549

≈

Ode to Captain Chesley B. Sullenberger

Scheduled to leave on a trip.
One final stop
the Danville, California library
to select a companion for flight.

The book-- "A Just Culture: Balancing Safety and
Accountability"
not an odd, casual reading choice
for a deadhead trip
for a man with whom the term 'deadhead'
could never be associated.

On the flight over
he read a few pages –
reflecting on his life
and where he had been.
Reserved – still fit and trim.
He had always done his job –
performed his role as a pilot and father
as life required.

Nestled into the Captain's chair at LaGuardia
the flight prepared
he read a few more pages.
Then slid the book into the console.

→

Airline Pilot, Hero of Flight 1549 – 2

≈

Thirty seconds into the flight
beyond hearing of the bird cannons
a flock of geese on a regular routine maneuver –
met his big bird.

In one of life's more poignant ironies –
both his bird and they, simultaneously meet their demise.
Less than a minute to summon all his skills and intellect
apply his instincts
succeed where no man had -
put steel to water
without the water prevailing.

In the end,
he helped them walk on water –
then the world thought he could as well.
Now called Hero...
The term suggests an act beyond his means.
To him –
just a job performed
as life and circumstance demand.

A few days later
his table strewn with messages
and calls he should return.

Talking heads wanting his picture and words.
The President his presence.
The Super Bowl his stature.

He settled into his arm chair
put the phone to his ear and dialed
  the only call which he knew he must make.

"Hello, Danville Public Library"

**"This is Captain Sullenberger
I lost the book that I borrowed last week."**

≈

The Ball that Got Away

≈

Ode to Fatherhood
Emily, and Steve Monteforto

All of his life he had just been hoping
to catch a foul ball off a Phillies' bat.
As a kid he remembers sitting
in Section 514 with his Pop,
watching a boy his age, in 218,
make a clean catch, one off Rose's bat
no bunch of other little pack-rats,
scrambling around in the seats for a loose ball,
a perfect form catch
like he had been taught to make in right field.

All these years, nothing had come even close.
Hey, what's the probability anyway?
He knew the statistics, just
like he recalculated each Phillies' batting average
after the games.

There was once when his Pop and he
sat in the first row of the Upper Deck,
the ball came sailing towards them
and he knew, that if he reached over the railing,
stretched as far as his small frame
would permit, that he could have had a chance
to catch it. But he was intimidated by that railing,
and the height. Only tepidly extended his arm
just missed.

Today, 20 years later, his Pop is gone
he sat with his 3-year-old daughter
who wore a pink baseball cap.
He was sharing his memories with her -
and making her own,
when all of a sudden, he heard the crack
looked up and saw the ball heading his way
no time to put on the glove which he still carried with him.
He reached up and made a fatherly, bare
handed catch. He knew inside his heart
that this should mean as much to her, as to him.

She would be waiting for this he was sure
the way he had all his life.
His long time dream reached.

He took the prize and shared it with her
handing it over.
She turned, wanting to please her Pop
the same way a catch by him
would have swelled up pride in his own dad,
and with one mighty heave
tossed the ball back onto the field.

One, not a father, might have wondered about
this frustrating moment, unexpected turn.
A lifetime dream lost, irretrievably.
He, in fact, was proud,
hugged her to make this moment his own,
the joy in her face - proving to her Pop
that she could do it, was all that he needed -
from the Ball that Got Away.

≈

Spaces

≈

Can you leave a part of yourself in a place?
Not just any place, of course.
But some especial place.
There are a few spaces on this earth
     which have touched me at a special time.
The memories which they hold because of my companion.
Shelter provided in my solitude and loneliness.

But can you leave a part of yourself there?

Is there a way you can become
     a permanent part of a place?
Etched in its memory, as it is in yours?
Something which the winds of change
     and the sands of time cannot erode.
Throughout the ages,
men have sought to build monuments to themselves
     in those places which they have touched.
Some have endured.
Their architects and artists long since forgotten.
Perhaps never known.

As for me,
I will cherish being just one more pebble on the beach,
     known only to myself
     and the one who loves me enough
       to have placed me there.
And this one act, and that small stone in a big place,
     will mean everything to me – I – having lost myself –
in the place.

The Last Thing He Wanted

≈

The last thing he ever wanted was to be a character in a
melodrama.
He sat at the edge of his bed, as if it was the edge of life,
and stared ahead into his past.

The open bottle of spirits, dispirited him – as it had for
years.

He had searched for himself in many things,
In many places he had found nothing and lost himself.

Longing only for a moment of understanding.
To take a wretched self
stand atop a hill and see something –
        instead of the chasm which summoned him.

To the depths he had plummeted
plunged headlong into the abyss of empty resonance.
Now desolate, pitiful...
Prepared to step at last into the endless silence
        where all retreat, but not at their own time.

Marching to his own drummer,
the constant din of senselessness
had beat until the temples of his head
became the altar upon which he sought rest.

But he had never wanted to be a character in a
melodrama....

The Man Without a Country

≈

The old gray coat which his daughter had given him for his
       birthday had worn thin.
It barely covered his self-respect, and was thread-bare
against the cold.

He found his way to this spot -
This man without a name
on a street without an address
from a family without a soul
in a country without a heart.

There is a grate on 42nd Street
which today is his one place of connection.
But the postman cannot find him
for the letters not written,
by the tearless who do not remember.

On the bench in Central Park
discarded by the uncaring
he reads the <u>Wall Street Journal</u>
before he stuffs it in his shoes
to replace his socks
lost not in the crash of '87 or '08
but somewhere between Roosevelt and the Parkway
to another unnamed and unknown
who took them for gloves.

Each day he walks -

From here to there.
From there to nowhere.
From this place to that.
To no place in particular.

On his way we pass him.
Shambling on our way -
From here to there.
From there to nowhere.
From this place to that.
To no place in particular.

One week he walked to Philadelphia along the Old York
Road
trod by presidents and commoners
to sleep inside one of six new empty
            cardboard refrigerator boxes
on the steps of the Federal Reserve Bank
            of the United States of America.
But he could not shame us;
besides the Eagles beat the Cowboys that day.

Yesterday we stepped over him.
Today the conscienceless step away from him,
as if the distance from street side to street side
will protect the heartless from the hardness which lies
from where there is no distancing.

→

The Man Without a Country – 3

≈

Is there anything in this man
of which to mark?
His being speaks not of his own essence,
but more of what is of us -
Who cannot take pity – or will not act upon it,
in a country which cannot cry.

One day he will recline upon the grate.
the next to not awake.
And the Times will little record
This sign of our times,
This passing which does not pass.

His coming and going soon forgotten.
Death having etched only this headstone:

**The man without a home
is also
a man without a country.**

Monet

Great Pond, Maine

≈

I know not much of art.
Nor of beginning,
      nor person whose energy bursts forth
      so silently upon the canvas.

I wonder now
      as I canoe beyond the bend
      of this small isle in a Great Pond
      why I see Monet in the trees and shoreline,
      etched from nature's palette upon the lake top.

Did he sit one day
      and feel the vibrant sun,
      the colors of the wind,
      in this rippling mirror on the world?

Or within the waters of his mother's womb
      did a call have its genesis,
      then silently touched the wall with brilliance
      where my gaze marvels on a life?

As I paddle through the painting of my mind
I wonder what was written on the side of the canoe
      in which he took the bend.

Sancta Sanctorum

≈

Rome, Italy

The Emperor Constantine's mother, St. Helena
had Pontius Pilate's steps
brought to Rome in the year 326 AD
a documented version of archaeological theft.

Now reinstalled across the Piazza
from Sans Giovanni in Laterano,
the church of popes.

No human foot may touch
-        the 28 white marble risers
-        the Scala Santa.
Wooden boards installed above,
grooves worn deep by pilgrims
who ascend on their knees in silent prayer
struggling to follow the path of Christ.
to acknowledge the human travail of the Deity's
trip to mortal condemnation.

At the top, the Chapel of the Holy of Holies,
        - the Sancta Sanctorum
where only the Pope may enter to pray...

Tell me, if only the Pope may enter....
does he take a squirt bottle of Windex with him
and clean the fingerprints off the inside
of the bullet proof glass?

Or is there a nun, who enters quietly
at 3 am to clean,
when the doors to the Chapel of St. Lawrence are shuttered,
the calm darkness of the night has fallen over the city
pilgrims and the clerics resting
having completed their reflection
on the day and on their God.....?

If a sister does visit to clean,
what does God say to her
when she asks him to pick up his feet?

≈

Market Street Mission

≈

Mike died overnight at the Market Street Mission.

To be more precise,
they stuck a shiv somewhere into the seven true ribs,
costae verae,
probably between rib 3 and 4.

Quietly his warm red blood
spilled across the cold floor –
through the thin mattress
which he had returned to each night
　　　for the last week.
A gray wool blanket matted frozen to his chest
when Sam tried to awake him that morning.

No one looked too hard for a murderer –
70 men had come and gone that evening and morning
　　　and each was capable of this act when the spirits
moved them.

The police were casual for the same reason.
Perfunctory.
70 suspects and 70 witnesses each with the same address:
This place – the Market Street Mission – yet no place.
None of them were in,
　　　literally and figuratively.

Even the innocent ones weren't so innocent.
Few would be able to identify their first-name-only fellow
travelers

despite the fact they shared the same haunts, day and night,
> never really seeing each other.

As the medical examiner's team lifted Mike onto the gurney
> and loaded him into the black bag
something dropped from his clinched fist
which the officers should have discovered - if they cared to look.

Last night, as with every evening,
Mike slept clutching his Marworth medallion
> just as he clutched his crucifix each evening as a
young boy.

"Lord, Grant me the serenity to accept the things I cannot change –
The courage to change the things I can-
and the wisdom to know the difference", read the inscription.

You see, no one freely chooses death when life and hope are an option.

Mike was a five-timer –
Carrier, Alina Lodge, Caron and Marworth twice. –
The last time he got kicked out for wrapping himself in bandages
> as would a sophomore in a college joke.

→

Market Street Mission – 3

≈

An airline pilot, he found the thread
that would weave his death in the Air Force in Afghanistan,
where, while burning off a field of mature Poppies
the aroma triggered a hidden gene he could not control –
later fed by the morphine administered to get him past the
shrapnel.

Tonight his mother would cry again – but not over today's
death.
No one knew Mike's last name
and with his last known address only: "Market Street
Mission",
they could not call her.
She had cried over his death a thousand times already,
the living passing away that took him.
She cried until the tears ran dry – and then she cried again.

A month later the Sergeant would find the fingerprint card
tossed aside in a stack of papers.
When submitted, it marked a hit
in the Department of Defense data base.
Someone notified his mother and dispatched a proper
escort
with his Purple Heart,
which he had neglected to pick up, or tell anyone about.

The examiner's attendant placed the Medallion back in his
hand
and folded the fingers tightly.

With a little luck the coin would be overlooked and
he would be buried with it in the potter's field.
When they exhumed the body at his mother's request
her purple heart would shatter yet again
when the undertaker handed her
the medallion of hope Mike carried,
on the evening when all hope was finally snuffed out.

At 1 pm that afternoon Mr. KT awoke in the park 4 blocks
away.
He casually ignored the blood on his hands.
He had seen it before, probably from scrounging around the
        dumpster in back of a restaurant.

He stumbled to the water fountain, took a drink and began
to scrub -
        blood off his hands
        and from his Marworth Medallion
        which he had slept holding last night.

You see, no one freely chooses murder when life and hope
        are an option.

When finished, he wondered what was for dinner that
evening
        at the Market Street Mission.

≈

Itinerant Poet

≈

He arrived early and signed the reading list.
Then sat comfortably in uncomfortable plastic chairs.
Familiar with the routine,
he would listen to the featured poet –
forming all the time, thoughts about his own writing.

He wrote from heartache or tragedy,
of some uncertain event or desire,
his inner hopes,
those darkest fears -
feelings for which paper and pen were conceived.
He could hide himself in the words,
like a child in a wood's thicket.
Though they all knew from his dew drop tears,
the quiver in his voice,
the emotional life center from which conceived.

The words he kept in plastic sleeves purchased at Staples
so the edges of his life's travails would not fray.
Others thought he ought once in awhile
change these glassine windows to his soul,
when the view was smudged from the caresses of finger
tips.

Once he may have thought more -
but after a lingering term,
he realized he wrote, but for himself.
People rarely asked him to come back – specifically.
Occasionally a novice high schooler
would come up to him afterwards

swept up in the emotion - not so much the words.
His style mimicked their high school writing
the unrequited love of the teenager
for the desk next door in English class.

Most gave up after two or three times,
or two or three months at the most –
some wondered why they even thought to come and read –
For each though, their precious symphony of words
composed for heartstrings
accomplished its purpose -
emotions now settled and merged into life's existence.

But he –
he, never quit --

When he died his tombstone should have read:

"Here lies an Itinerant Poet.
He persevered.
His words comforted him.
He caressed them
as he slept the one last time."

→

Itinerant Poet - 3

≈

His daughter took the plastic sleeves,
placed them by the headstone,
put a small stone upon them,
covered them with leaves.

He as a bystander, would have written about her feelings.
Her touching sentimental acknowledgment
of these deep emotional companions - that spoke of him.

He would have wished though, they had at least made
copies.
If he knew, he would have preferred they saved them -
even if it was in a dusty attic where no one
would find them except the moving company.
He would have chosen that a cleaning man
be the one to throw them away.

Now they belonged to the wind and the elements
        -- as did he.

≈

More Bars than Anyplace Else

≈

"No one has more bars than us"
broadcast the billboard
on Route 18 in New Brunswick, NJ,
which initially I thought
had to be a promotion
of the Hoboken Chamber of Commerce.

Old haunts of Hoboken.
A bar on every corner
the natives knew the name of each
hard-working Germans, Irish, Italians, Yugoslavs
spent the hours after the shift whistle blew
tipping beers, watching the end of the Yankees" game
on fuzzy black-and-white screens
ogling the waitresses
and worse.

Then as night fell in the streets
they had sense enough to go home
to build strength for the next day's work--
or found young sons
sent to the taverns by mothers
whose dinners were cooling on the table.

First the jobs went.
Then the Longshoremen followed.
Then the bar stools stood eerily empty,
→

≈

only an occasional traveling Fuller brush salesman
trying to swallow his pride
along with his Scotch.

Selling brushes was an important job -- but was not work,
real work was something a man did with his hands.

Then they decided the bars should go the way
of the working man.
Slink into oblivion.
So the lawyers were unleashed
bartenders designated diagnosticians.
Replace the customers' mothers
and shoo the patrons away
when they had had too much.

Young sons could no longer be sent to the bar
to make the dinner call.
They were in school -- building character
through organized sports, singing in the choir
playing the tuba in the marching band
not home tinkering in the wooden cubicled basements
of the Hoboken tenements.

So the bars closed.
The yuppies moved in.
They renamed the bars "taverns"
and put fancy prices and names on the drinks
martinis named after insects and fruit

weak sugar-coated alcohol
carrying not too oblique, sexually suggestive names
like:
-- bangers
-- in between the sheets
-- naked ladies
-- and the names of bras and panties.

The docks replaced with office towers
-        and condominiums.
No one knew if the money was real
the computers exchanged it, no one saw it.
Inside the packed bars
they held cell phone to their ears,
or kept little earpieces on all evening
as they finessed each other
and tried to seduce a trip to childless lofts.
No families to support
just habits.

Each looked--
as they entered a new establishment
for how many bars the cell phone bore,
not realizing that they need not look far--
since in Hoboken there has always been
a bar on every corner--
more bars than anyplace else.

Birdhouses

≈

Why do we build birdhouses,
when for years birds have been able to take care of
themselves?

For generations, since the time they were dinosaurs,
birds have nested.

If they were still dinosaurs,
I could understand how they could need help building
dinosaur houses.

But birdhouses?

And who decides what colors
each birdhouse resident really likes?

Why do people feel that birds like colors on their houses,
that humans would never paint their own?

Is this paint leftover from something?
Discarded in the 60's
from a psychedelic road show.

Now dog houses I understand.
I have never seen a dog build a house.

So why do we build
Birds,
Houses,
when they can do it themselves?

Does anyone really know?

La Ragazza (The Girl) Behind the Tent Flap

≈

L'Aquila, Italy
April 2009
...earthquake

She peered out from behind the blue tent flap.
Just ten-years-old, her world had changed.

A bitter spring cold
a blue pull-over Croce Rossa Italiana knit hat
a white ski jacket
with a brilliant red execution post, with cross–bar, as the
breast plate
and a hood.

A young Pionieri stands by her side
tears streaming down his face,
like the rain which buffeted the rescue workers.

The girl knows these aren't her clothes.
Senses the world outside the tent flap,
no longer hers.

Her forlorn face
a vestment she would wear throughout her life
and on her wedding day...
no father to walk her down the aisle
nor mother to help her with her gown.
Mother earth had swallowed her Italian town
starving the girl, left an orphan,
staring - peering out - from behind a tent flap.

→

La Ragazza (The Girl) Behind the Tent Flap -2

≈

They say on the day Christ died,
the earth also shook, opened up
and the dead walked in and out of life.
Why were they awakened?
Were their deaths transformed
as was the life of this young girl?

If not, why trouble this preziosa bambina?

The night before, no sense of impending doom
Italian mothers and their altar boys
knelt in silent prayer,
expecting little – only parental protection,
and the sun to rise in the morning.
Why were their prayers left unanswered?
This tragedy, a shallow response
to sincere respect, and innocent dependency.

So – we, and they now vagabonds –
traverse these scenes.
Life not defined by when, and how, death calls -
or why we live,
or when we have our time of suffering - behind the tent
flap.

Tragedies, neither deliberate nor designed
are to be as life chooses, or not.
No prayer of supplication can set a road block
barrier.
They come as the passing freight train,
as the sun moves east to west.

Life's purpose measured
only by our observation from the wayside -
and whether we offer a white coat with a hood
to the girl behind the tent flap.

≈

"My Father's Hands" – **page 86**

(by Teresa Alessandria De Sapio of TADS-Art & Illustration)

IV

My Father's Hands

≈

I looked down when I awoke
and saw I had my father's hands.

Last night,
my own slipped comfortably into my gloves.
Would these?
For years I thought I could not fill his shoes.

These hands I now possess are so familiar.
When I was young
I'd watch them try to mold my being --
shape the changing silhouette
which would one day
a shadow cast upon the world.

A constant presence –
from the time I saw them pick me up -
comfort me – dust me off –
point me in the right direction –
and push me on my bicycle ride to manhood.

Powerful, I observed them work and grip –
hew the measure of the wood
tighten, screw, and lift –
meet and master every challenge.

At the table of our sustenance, reassuring.
Clenched in an evening prayer of thanks -
and of anxiety I did not see.

Derisively I wondered
why he could not clean below his fingertips.

Occasionally he crafted
          a brief note with a #2 lead pencil.
Though his hands spoke more meaningfully in other ways –
always in control.

Now as he fumbled
          with the buttons of his pajama top,

I used these gifts of inheritance
          to thread the unfastened loopholes –
and gently gripped the trembling hands which parented me
          to pull him up from his recliner.

He did not want to let go –

          a feeling I remember from my youth.

≈

Mother's Day

≈

She looks now from the hillside.
The view is calming, the early morning sunrise
warms the green grass,
shakes the dew from its slumber
asks it to move along.
Deer visit in the evening.
The flowers her children plant draw their attention.

She still looks forward to Mother's Day.
They visit then again
pull the weeds which the deer ignore,
having weeded their own souls -
visiting Mom does that.

She will enjoy seeing them and the grandchildren
all dressed up for church
heartwarming memories of past Mother's Days,
when all the hard work looked so pretty.

In heaven they have not resolved
whether to let mothers
have a continuing view of their children's lives.
They've tested it, much too emotional -
emotion the one great gift that they don't take
when you pass.

So this day Mom gets to see only the best -
savors pride which lingers on the hillside

like the sweet smell of the lilacs, growing along the woods'
edge,
wafts through the warming air.

Her youngest comes alone in the evening twilight
to sit and watch the deer eat his mother's fresh flowers.
He was the only one who knew she found the deer beautiful
-
and did not mind when they ate the shrubs in the backyard.

≈

Running with Scissors

≈

I was tempted the other day,
to run with scissors,
just to prove to my mother
that I could do it safely.

Though I am 35 and she has been gone 10 years
I still cannot do it.

I fear that as she warned,
I would trip and pierce my heart
or gouge my eye out.
Worst yet, I could fall and drive it into the dirt
and dull its sharpened edges
much to my mother's irritation.

A priest had warned me once
of being with a girl unless I was married.
When I made young love the first time
I thought for sure I would die.
I have made love many times since.

But I still cannot run with scissors.

An Old Forgotten Book

≈

In a stack, in a room
where dust knows no bounds
in the library,
where their idea is to rent DVD's
of Mork and Mindy reruns -
lies an old forgotten book.

It called out to me one day
as I walked past -
the raglan blue cover
gold embossed words on the spine.
I needed to stop and bend over,
and peer closely to read.

The binding at the top was worn
actually torn from the numerous times
where it was opened and closed,
when it had a value
when it was so coveted
the time one could keep it as a companion
was strictly limited -
one paid a fine for depriving another
of its words.
Now I could probably walk off with it - and never return.
The library might even feel I was doing it a favor
freeing up space for its new wing
of video game rentals.

→

An Old Forgotten Book - 2

≈

Inside its cover was still a cardboard pocket,
a slot where its journeys could be traced -
like the GPS now records
where my car and I have been -
voluntary or not.

I lift the card and find a name -- Elijah Pringle
and the date: September 14, 1954.
Could it be 50 years have passed

since hands last touched this paper,
folded open the pages,
saw the words take life in the imagination of the mind?
What does the author think now?
Does he look down
and wonder whether anyone will open its pages again?

Elijah -- Elijah Pringle,
where did these words once consumed carry you?
Did they impart wisdom
or relaxation
or stimulate a mind to one great deed,
or prompt one small kindness?

I think I will borrow this book
if it is not now too old and fragile
for the journey to my home -
and like the elder one

I volunteer to take outside
on Saturdays from the nursing home
I'll treat this long forgotten book
with care,
and hope the attention that I pay to it
will not be its demise.

I fear that when they find these stray old ones
they will not re-shelve them
but sell them instead at the next book fair
to raise money for their borrow a book on-line program
where somehow the pages self-destruct
after two weeks on your computer screen,
no fines are levied
no more shelves, no more dark blue raglan covers
just memories of the words in my mind.

≈

Sagebrush

≈

Thoughts ramble through my mind
    like the sagebrush of time.

Yet with all this thinking
    wisdom is still elusive.
Thoughts become tangled in barbed wire fences
    never intended for an open range.

This sagebrush...

Its grayish, green leaves
    cast an aromatic fragrance through the still night air.
A cooking herb, once the home of the sage grouse -
The grouse having left no wiser for the nesting...
    learned but no longer sage.
Now the small white flowers having fallen
    -- as all must.

My mind...

Gray matter too is food for thought.
Sustenance of life,
    essence of death.

Wrestling thoughts
is like embracing saguaro.
A prickly dilemma
    is what mankind was designed for...

Or is it destined for?

The Coach's Whistle

≈

Draped with ceremony
over the doorknob
of the closet of his retirement
the whistle and its lanyard
jostled and blown for the last time after 18 years.
It -- deserved better than to be hidden in a box
or a drawer some place.

It -- carried memories.
Boxes are very rarely a good place
for memories which are to be used regularly,
rather than only awakened when house cleaning.

So the knob on this closet door
seemed like a place of fitting tribute.
Each morning and each evening
he would hear it clank incongruously against the wood
as he folded and unfolded the bi-fold door
to place and retrieve his coat.

Would he get to blow it one last time –
summon the chargers of youth,
or would death blow its whistle before he had the chance?

How to Eat a Cannoli

≈

Cannoli won second place
for the dessert with the worst eating design
second only to a hot dipped, thin-coated,
chocolate covered soft vanilla ice cream cone
on an August summer's day.

I understand why
they have to see through both ends of the shell
when filling it up -
but why would anyone design a dessert
which, when you bite on one end,
you lose 25% of the equivalent of the dessert out the other?

Now a Hot Dog.
There's a functional cylindrical type food.
The dog tucked cozily in the bun.
When you chew on one end you do not loose
mustard, relish and onions out the other.
Compare that to a Big Mac.
Bite at any one point and you have drippings drama
around all of the edges.

The cannoli's problem would be almost tolerable
if you were losing just mayonnaise, ketchup or mustard
or that messy combination of goo that
soothes your hamburger taste buds.

But cannoli filling is Italian health food
the whole cow's milk ricotta cheese
dark milk chocolate chips
(and whatever else is in there)
the sweet nectar of life.

I ate dinner once with an American
who thought he'd solve the problem with a knife and a fork
attempting to daintily cut through the shell
in order to pick up pieces.
Cutting through a cannoli shell!
"gat outa here"!

If they wanted you to break the shells apart
they would have crushed them up for you
and sprinkled them on top of the filling
and served them to you with a plastic spoon
in one of those paper cups for pansies.

There is only one way to eat cannoli.
Bite on one end
and as far as the other end goes -
"Fuhgeddaboudit..."

≈

Regret

≈

I forgot to tell her that I loved her.
Long enough for her to forget that she loved me.
Busying myself with busy things
I hurried past daylight.
The sunlight glistening on my back
brightening the path which I did not follow.

Having learned,
what good is this knowledge?

Why only now, too late,
so long, so foolish, so lost...
do I perceive
what love's best's nature tells true love?

Perhaps regret, like love,
is meant as one of life's better sentiments.

Better to regret, and have lost –
then never to regret at all.

The Darkness

≈

The darkness is a good place for lonely people.

Very accommodating.

You need not see yourself, or others.
No one will find you, so long as you are quiet.

You will be left alone; won't be bothered.

It sounds good.

So tell me, why are you afraid?

The Meadow of My Soul

We walked again across the meadow of my soul.
The green grass trimmed comfortably for our bare feet.
Just a few patches of brown, from my earlier years.
Not enough for her to be concerned.
The larger swaths tidied up and covered with brush
　　　to hide my embarrassment.

On a late spring day like this – those spots can hardly be
noticed.
It is in the winter, when the delicate snow falls,
when the ground is still warmer than the chill air,
then - the white shines brilliantly, glistens in the sunlight.
It is then, that the bare spots stand out clearly.
Though up and until this time, only I walk here that time of
year.

When concerned,
they told me God looks at this place
from high up above
and from that vantage sees only the broad expanse.
If that is the case, he must be pleased – isn't he?

We have not journeyed together to her meadow.
At times I wonder why she has not invited me.
But I am not concerned.
Her meadow is just through a small patch of woods up
ahead.
I'm sure we will talk – and walk there someday.
Anyway, I have always feared whether I could behave
myself
　　　in that tempting wood.

My Thoughts Escaped Me

≈

As I yawned my thoughts escaped me.
Involuntarily trapped within my wishful thinking,
I'd kept them prisoners, lest my companions
        appreciate I was someplace else.

Now summoned by my boredom,
        some audible phrase of 3 to 4 words
        left my brain and ventured into the airways of
        human discourse
to be treated disdainfully by my associates,
        adsorbed in their own words –
        startled by my yawn to begin with.

Having intentionally been ignored
        my thoughts travelled on the words,
        through the air,
as if on the foot of a carrier pigeon.

On the way, they found shelter from a storm
within the beams of a barn
        atop a field of once cut hay,
where he reached up before the pigeon could alight
        and grasped the words within his calloused hands,
        and contemplated the thoughts
as he directed the horses of the hay wagon
through the hillside fields, now fallow –

Where the thoughts were lost,
        as he unloaded the bales onto the stack.

And somewhere in the farm fields of Iowa,
My thoughts lie crushed between two bales.
Fodder for a mushroom farm in the adjacent county.

"Walking ATM" – page 108
(by Teresa Alessandria De Sapio of TADS-Art & Illustration)

V

Pins

≈

On his lapel, stood pins of distinction.
Signaling fame, however ephemeral
    cast in the communality of the iron of endurance
    bred by those who walked before him.

He did not know them.
In fact, many have long since been forgotten.
As will he, when his pins are left discarded
    in a tiny felt lined box
    in the attics of memory
    where the nuisances of unimportance
    are moved with a shambling gate
    from one corner to another.

Then one day, the curiosity of youth stumbled upon the box
–
Blew the dust into the air, opened the lid
    and aired the memories of forgotten ideals
    cast aside by the arrogant certainty of purpose,
    so much a part of the youth's father.

The grandson's eyes lit up with undoubting gleam –
    the brilliance of hope – of endurance beyond
adversity.
He grasped the pins and wore them to school the next day –
    and into the school yard.

From thence, he set his course as if for mankind
     to achieve some deed beyond his means.
As he grew, he treasured those ideals and pins.
Walked steadfast in his grandfather's footsteps with pride.

For humanity he eventually touched this terrestrial sphere
ever so
     perceptibly.
When he breathed his last sigh, they placed the pins on his
lapel
     and put a folded flag at his fingertips.
Before they closed the lid, his son removed the pins –
     and they gave him the flag.

And - as was the custom - with complacent smugness and
disdain -
the pins were thereafter sold at the next garage sale.

≈

I only eat on Fridays

≈

**50,000 people die of hunger each day.
A child, every 5 seconds.**

Every 5 seconds,
as the world devours a McDonald's french fry -
starvation consumes a child.

The path to this destination of death – contorted.

At first, pains of hunger turn to numbness
then tissue thin skin
clings to the skeleton, like a balloon out of air
falls amongst the netting on the circus floor
below the high wire of life….

In Costa Rica, 53 years old,
he trudges for the 40th consecutive year,
the 14,600th consecutive day to the refuse dump
where he fights with the other human scavengers – and the
rats
for rotten, left over morsels to sustain his family.

When the garbage truck arrives, a rush like lemmings
or vermin avoiding the exterminator
to be the first - push to the front
when the dump body releases rotting, days old food.

Sheltered in a tin covered lean-to,
an anxious family awaits
having returned from a difficult walk
to the stream below
- where people

bathe, drink, urinate, defecate
and catch amoebic dysentery.

Upon his return, his pickings,
food scraps parceled out among family members
each - with their own day of the week to eat.

In the intervening days,
when the growls pull on the heartstrings of a mother -
when the cries can no longer be tolerated
she mixes clay with salt and water -
a paste more suitable for a child's nursery school project,
and bakes dirt pies -
so the stomachs of her children feel full.

On the beach at the resort -
with the white colored sand, the crystal blue waters,
under the green trimmed cabana
the ocean waves lullaby my afternoon's end.
I invite an emaciated urchin to share
half a local unfinished sandwich,
one the restaurant's garbage purveyor can do without.

I offer it up
encourage this thin replica of a human child
to pick it from the plate -
tears from the child's eyes -
at first - I thought appreciation
but when he still resisted,
my inquiry answered:

"This is Thursday, and I only get to eat on Friday...

Friday is my day to eat....."

Walking ATM

≈

"The New Colossus"
Emma Lazarus

New York 1886

In the harbor stands a lady.
Liberty Enlightening the World.
La liberté éclairant le monde, 1886
Mother of Exiles.
Ardor burning boldly in a torch,
emblazoned on a bronze plaque:

> **"Give me your tired, your poor,**
> **Your huddled masses yearning to breathe free,…"**

Millions accepted that standing invitation
steerage paid for with pennies saved
from an honest day's work
sent home by parents and relatives
who built the cities of their destination,
and the steamships which carried them.

Now the landed inteligencia,
having reaped the harvest of their roots
argue the meaning ascribed and its relevance today –
while the "illegals" tend their lawns,
pick the oranges and tomatoes,
turn the hamburgers
and brew their morning coffee after an evening
of cleaning their offices.

"The wretched refuse of your teeming shore.
Send these, the homeless, tempest-tost to me,.."

<u>They</u> trudge in the footsteps of the ancestors of the debaters,
spurned for belief - seeking relief from prejudice –
poverty, joblessness, epidemic,
famine, potatoes rotting in the fields,
dictators' wars.
These fueled the engines of their passage.

The Journey to freedom…America's embryonic gift…
to those whose lineage or feudal state melded not
into countries without a melting pot.

Today they come,
to do the work Americans need,
but feel below them –
but not below those who come from down below.

<u>New Orleans 2007</u>

<u>He</u> – walked – rode - and swam…
      into the city of death,
      when no one cared who entered
      just who left.

For two weeks, in a dark, damp, fetid,
sardined packaged cargo container,
no longer a carrier for New Orleans exports,
now transporting human cargo from Honduras to New Orleans.

→

Walking ATM – 3

≈

He congregated at the day workers' hiring hall
in the parking lot of the vacant boarded up
"On the Run" convenience store on Elysian Fields Avenue.

The irony lost on him, when two years later
the American Vietnamese moved back,
the store reopened, the New Orleans police were called
to push the proud supplicants away,
as if they, who did the cleanup, needed to be cleaned up.
Transformed into the refuse they picked.

"I lift my lamp beside the golden door."

He too sent cash back –
but not to those hoping to join him.
The golden door to America now bolted shut.

The wetback, *mojado,* paid in greenbacks again today –
confronted on the broken sidewalk to the Western Union
office
by the human refuse of America.

Too arrogant to work, they plied their trade
preying on those with names they chose not to pronounce,
each only "Hey, Jose."

A lead pipe signaled an end to his American dream.
They were heard to remark:

"Another f...ing Walking ATM."

New York Times –
2/18/1883
Immigrants via New
Orleans

New Orleans, Feb. 17. – The steam-ship Paris, of the French Commercial Line, arrived here yesterday from Havre with 20 French and Italian immigrants, ticketed through to San Francisco via the Southern Pacific and her Louisiana and Texas connections. The cost from starting-point to destination is about $80 per passenger. This is the first lot of immigrants sent from Europe by this route, but it is believed it will be adopted hereafter. The immigrants left by the train with no further delay than was necessary to pass the Custom-house.

New York Times -
2/15/2009
Day Laborers Are Easy
Prey in New Orleans

New Orleans – They are the men still rebuilding New Orleans more than three years after Hurricane Katrina, the head-down laborers from Honduras, Mexico and Guatemala who work on the blazing hot roofs and inside the fetid homes for a wad of cash at the end of the day. But on the street, these laborers are known as "walking A.T.M.'s."

Washed Up Attorney

≈

They called him "that old curmudgeon."
The young bucks in their $1500 hand tailored Italian suits.
Their Bruno Maglis spit and shined,
they stood like peacocks astride the courtroom bar
and talked of cars and trips and hot paralegals,
discussions which would be continued that Friday evening
     at the bar at The Taproom.

He sits in silence mid-way in the courtroom,
     tucked in the left hand side near the isle.
He could never endure sitting in the middle of a row.
Barely noticed, he surveyed a scene
     he had watched from this vantage point for a
generation –
     he, himself, no longer watched or noticed.

The case is called
     and they move quickly through the railing gate
     to their table where they unpack.
Remove the wads of paper pleadings
     generated in volume by the high tech tools
     of their paperless society.
Their laptops unholstered with their wireless connections -
in case the computers have previously forgotten something
     which the lawyers
     had never thought was their responsibility
     to think about to begin with.

He removed a frayed yellow legal pad
     from the battered satchel

which, he would admit, he one day shined as vigorously
        as they now shine their shoes.

They went first, as they would insist, and
        regaled the judge with quotes and citations
        and obscure affidavits from irrelevant
        "witnesses" who saw nothing -- but thought they
had.

Smugly they rested as he arose slowly.

With succinct words and surgical precision
        he sliced and diced their argument
        and left the entrails on their counsel table
        so they could read the signs when court adjourned.

Jaws dropped and locked, they quickly looked down at
        their Blackberries as if their Wizards of Oz would
        save them from behind their black screens.

As the judge spoke, the reasoning of his ruling
        rang through hollow ears.
What alibi would they concoct
for being vanquished by a washed up lawyer?
They texted their offices
to churn the money making engines of appeal.

He turned and almost shuffled toward the courtroom door,
his scarf drooping unceremoniously from his pocket.
He did not stop for the traditional meaningless banter,
where the victor gloated while seeming not to,

→

Washed Up Attorney – 3

and the other side exchanged pleasantries while whispering
        "you son of a bitch"
under their breath.

This too had changed since his time,
when the courtroom was not a steel cage
but a light stand where they all welcomed the truth.

If he had waited they would not have spoken to him
anyway.
"Old" is defined in Black's Law dictionary as "ignored" –
no Blackberry – no intellect.

He had been in the elevator many times
when the constant buzz of the electronic tethers
set on silent, silently drove you crazy by their vibration
while talking over each other -
a cacophony of argument with black boxes.

The door to the entry foyer slid open.
Across the floor he stopped at the place
        that through the years
        provided some reality in a world of incongruous
imagery.

He opened the door to the janitor's closet,
pulled up a plastic chair,
accepted an encrusted mug of coffee
        and spoke to the only man
whose companionship in the courthouse
had meant anything for 30 years.

The Poet's Hands at Twilight

≈

These hands are like the satin edges
        of a new born baby's blanket
tucked tenderly beneath the future
swaddling the present through the night.

Resting infant.
Comforted from the night's dark shadows
sheltered from the world's worries
by these hands of protection –

Hands at rest
at the edge of a weary day
one placed on top of the other
wondering what the next will bring.

Now grasp loosely, but firmly, a pencil
to play yet a silent poet's score
on the back of an envelope
        from the credit card company.

He Died with His Spikes On

≈

In tribute to Le Roy "Lee" Hammer
Livingston, NJ
1920-2006

The lady from down the street,
when I meet her someplace
an elementary school friend
asked about him.

"He always had his baseball uniform on,"

**"Day and night as we played in the neighborhood
it was a part of him
as much as his hands,"**

"I wondered whether he slept in it,".

Baseball.
His was a generation of baseball.
A generation that traded cards
and their uniforms for those of their Country
while their mothers cried at home
whenever they looked in their closets—

They played pickup games while waiting to ship out
nap sacks as bases
then cleaned up for horrors so bleak
that they returned to never talk about it,
used silent hand signals from the bench
known only to each other
and not those in the stands.

He took stenographic notes
of the trials of those who ran the wrong way
then faced firing squads for the sake of the team
cried at night –
although baseball players are not supposed to cry.

He returned to become a Livingston NJ diamond,
coached Legion Ball and taught boys of summer
how to become men, face life,
and use the correct parts of speech.

After the field, the Legion Hall was his third base
an unspoken fraternity where they sat
wondered without saying
what they had been through
still balked about talking about it,
even to each other,
watched the Yankees and listened to Mel Allen
he waited for when the Pirates were in town.

I wish I could have been there
instead of a safety patrol for the school bus
in Baptistown, New Jersey when
in the 60's series
Virdon's ball hit a little stone
popped the Adam's Apple in Kubek's tree,
→

He Died with His Spikes On – 3

≈

then Mazeroski smashed one over the fence.
I cried – though I am sure he had that wry little smile
of satisfaction, one of the few times the Pirates
lived up to their name and stole something.

"So, did you ever hear about the golfer
who needed two pair of pants
in case he got a 'hole in one'?",
he asked the first time he meet me.

Those that he touched
filed past
knowing that like the cowboys of old,
he, for certain,
died with his spikes on.

≈

When the End is Near

≈

When you know the end is near.
When the combat has ended.
And time shows how unimportant
          - important things were.
When old enemies prove to be human.
When prospective
          - paints hues to old truths.

When you meet an enemy, aged,
          -coming out of the hospital elevator.
When you yourself have lost your hair
          - to chemotherapy.
When eyes blur the reasons for battle
          - along with the battlefield.

When time forgets what the argument was all about.

Then you reminisce for a moment about head strong youth.
Laugh, then hug as you depart –
          - a small tear in the corner of your eye.

Knowing this will be the last gesture
          - the battles now concluded
Already forgotten, remembered only
          - in the annals of respect.

A Window with the Sunshine

≈

I want to sit in a window with the sunshine.

When I grow old, that's all I want –
A restaurant window in the sunshine.

My friend, the cherished actor
had his choice of any seat his fame desired.
The maître d' prepared a quiet table in the corner.
Privacy from peering eyes and boisterous strangers.

But for all his years in the limelight,
He sought only one thing –
A window in the sunshine.

More than fresh air –
the generous rays of warmth
envelope a personality, etch calm in body and soul.
Solace in elder years.

I harkened back to my younger days.
A quiet table in a dark corner, dim lights,
comforted and provided security for me
and the one I loved.

And then in middle years, a table twice removed, assuaged my
ego.
Assured me of my importance.
Sheltered me from the very fame I sought.

And now....and now....

As the tide of life recedes,
I want to sit in a window with the sunshine.

Old is Where I Left You,
the Last Time We Danced

≈

We both remembered younger days
we moved with ease, glided smoothly across the floor
all eyes focused in our direction
your dress, your figure, your elegant stature
your presence graced the room
our feet untethered, alight on air.

The deep blue look in my eyes,
focused intently on yours.
I gaze, even when we were seated
no question, no doubt,
that we are in love.
Our dance painted the picture.

Now at age 75, in our 50th year of marriage
we happily struggle, shuffle our feet.
One slow dance around the polished floors of memory.
In a tender embrace,
aged to perfection through the years.
The soles of our shoes caress the wooden floors.
Still glide, though not effortlessly
carried by the melodies and memories.

We did not have to exchange words to know
we were not destined for Dancing with the Stars
but the stars in my eyes tell yet
of my love.

This - still our story.
Though - old is where I left you
the last time we danced.

Writer's Bump

≈

In elementary school
I had a writer's bump.
On the top upper side of my right middle finger.

I think it grew from squeezing my pencil
too hard and too long.

Do kids today get a writer's bump?
Or know what it, or even a pencil, is?
Have they both been replaced
with carpel tunnel syndrome?

Has the bump gone the way
of six foot snow drifts that we used to trudge in,
to and from school, both ways uphill?
and recess
and the milk bottle outside the front door in early morning
and marbles dropped in a shoe box hole
and simple times
and simple talks
uncomplicated friendships
simple games
and a prayer to start the day?

Do they take a shower after gym,
or do they do they even have it (gym or a shower)?
Parallel bars in dusty storage closets,
horses that today are used to sit on and smoke
when you can sneak in the basement.

Dresses with sleeves and backs
and underwear that stays under
pants with belts
lockers without locks
hallways without cell phones
and manners....
and good morning
and there is a reason to go home.

I remember the days when my writer's bump would swell
from drawing countless penmanship circles
thump a little from blood rushing through my veins.

Now I look down, realize it is gone,
I had almost forgotten it.

Could I have remembered it better than it was?
Failed to remember that it really, really hurt?
Forgotten why our parents thought we were a lost
generation.
Understand really –
that you cannot walk to, and from school,
both ways - uphill?
And it doesn't snow enough anymore anyway.

In my heart, I fear that kids today
miss the writer's bump more than I do.

≈

Your Favorite Piece

≈

When once an author was asked
which of his works he liked the best,
He replied,
"The one I am with at the time."

This struck the hearer strange.
Does not he have his favorite?
I know I do.

Until a passerby remarked:
"If I were to ask you,
'Which of your children do you like the best?'
What would be your reply?"

A Good Poem

≈

A good poem is like a good sermon –

It should have a good beginning.
Must have a good ending.

and both should be as close together as possible.

His Head Upon the Pillow

≈

The sun touched his check
tenderly -
softly, through the window pane.
It had arisen awhile ago
and now the alarm bells of the new day
called for him,
as the sun called for the earth –
to stir.

Somehow earlier,
in the darkness he had lost his pillow
his head now rested against the mattress
the sheet ruffled,
the pillow like a giant beanbag
wedged against the headboard.

He turned.
His wife had not stirred.
Sheltered from the sun's rays
for at least another 20 minutes.

He fluffed the pillow,
tilted his head
placed the feather down where a calm sleep
would have found it in the morning,
let it caress his neck.
Saturday granted him this indulgence.

It would be only 60 seconds until life
revoked the permission.
His mind, granted the blessing of a night's calm,
only the subconscious on watch,
now noticed the sun.
Those worries
which he had carried to the pillow the night before
were still there - alert, refreshed
and ready to face another day.

≈

Poems by Title – Alphabetic

→

≈

Poems by First Line

→

≈

Acknowledgments

Grateful appreciation is extended to the Editors of the following Journals or periodicals that have published or are about to publish poems from this book. Thank you.

The **New Jersey Lawyer Magazine** which published "Washed Up Attorney". (April 2009)

The **13th Annual Poetry Ink Chapbook**, Moonstone Publishing, Philadelphia, Pennsylvania which published "Lying in Wait". (April 2009)

The Star-Ledger of Newark, NJ and columnist Mark Di Ionno who substantially reproduced "Shoveling Snow on Wii". (March 2009)

The New Verse News (on-line) which published "I Learned to Kill for You (2/10) and "I only eat on Friday" (3/10)

"What's Your Exit (on-line)? A Literary Detour Through New Jersey" "More Bars than Anyplace Else" and "Mums" 3/10

The **14th Annual Poetry Ink Chapbook**, Moonstone Publishing, Philadelphia, Pennsylvania which published "I Learned to Kill for You". (April 2010)

PoetSpeak (on-line) "Talking Bed" (2/10)

"Market Street Mission" is to be published in the next edition of **The Big Hammer.**

"Running with Scissors" is to be published in the next edition of the **Edison Literary Review**.

"What Progress has Wrought" is to be published in **FreeXpresSion**, an Australian magazine.

"Monet" is to be published in the next edition of the **River Poets Journal**.

"I Learned to Kill for You" to be published in the next edition of **The River.**

Awards:

"The Last Thing He Wanted", was awarded a 2009 Recognition Award by the **New Jersey Poetry Society.** (April 2009)

WATCH FOR RAY BROWN'S

Collection of Poems for the Holidays

The Crèche

*available October 2010 on-line and
in bookstores everywhere*

The Title Poem

The Crèche

≈

When just a youth, the nativity crèche
held meaning beyond the limits of his young mind.
He played out the scenes with the figurines,
over and over -
the story never grew old.

His family's custom was to set the manger in early
December
leave the cow's trough empty,
young baby Jesus would await Christmas day to appear.

The privilege of placing the Christ child
in the real yellow straw
his father procured from a local farmer
meant more than even the six shooters and holster

Santa left him under the tree.
He vied with his sisters to be the one
to place the babe for the first time.

Each night thereafter
before he lay his head upon the pillow
he took the infant in his arms
placed a kiss upon His forehead,
said his evening prayers there, at the foot of the tree.

As with most teenage men
this scene held diminishing fascination.
As a young Harvard educated man
the story, not quite forgotten, but never repeated
lest his intellect be questioned.

The crèche soon a near forgotten memory
until at age 32, he, himself, had a babe for Christmas.
Somehow it seemed only right,
he not being totally an agnostic,
to place below the trimmed green tree
the figures of a family
and a lone cow to breath warmth.

As he set this scene emotions swelled,
he remembered younger days.
Father and mother now gone,
the comfort of their home
the warmth of his Christmas manger,
having disappeared.

→

The Crèche

≈

3

Placing the young Christ Child on top of the refrigerator
to await Christmas day,
he could not help but plant a kiss upon his forehead,
and when he laid his own head upon the pillow that evening
he wondered whether he should have it examined.
A 32 year old broker with a Harvard Masters
kisses the figurine of a young Babe
before he retires?

The next morning over coffee and the Wall Street Journal
he was distracted by the season
and when his wife arose to join him -
they had both long since stopped going to church -
he asked her what she thought about attending Midnight
Mass
at the local parish within walking distance, a block and one
half away,
if the evening was temperate they could wrap their own
babe
in swaddling clothes and share whatever Christmas warmth
this longing fulfilled would bring.

≈

FOLLOW RAY BROWN'S POETRY

Read his most current poetry:

The Poetry of Ray Brown --
   http://raybrown.wordpress.com

*Ray on **Facebook*** -- *http://tinyurl.com/RayBrownFanPage*

*Ray on **Twitter*** --
  *http:***//twitter.com/poetbrown**

*To purchase **"I Have His Letters Still"***
  http://poet-ray-brown.com

Purchase *"I Have His Letters Still"* at

*www.buybooksontheweb.com, Amazon, Borders and Barnes and Noble
on-line, other* online book sellers, your local bookstores and watch for it
on Kindle and Sony Readers.

Ray Brown
PO Box 40
Frenchtown, NJ 08825
poetraybrown@earthlink.net

Interior photos, cover photography, and wraparound design
by Teresa Alessandria De Sapio of TADS-Art & Illustration,
(plates pages j, 84, & 102)

About the Poet

Ray Brown lives in Frenchtown, New Jersey, 60 miles west of New York City and 50 miles north of Philadelphia, along the Delaware River.

His home is nestled on a ridge overlooking the Delaware River and the cliffs on the Pennsylvania side, a place for reflection and writing.

Ray has been writing for 20 years but until December 2008 had only shared his work with a handful of people. From time to time, when the mood struck he would write on the back of napkins, on reports in a business meeting, on index cards, in a little notebook, and then at times with less distractions on a computer. In December 2008 he set up a blog to share his work publicly.

He is a graduate of the University of Notre Dame and Rutgers-The State University of New Jersey.

His poetry has appeared in 13th and 14th Annual Poetry Ink Chapbook, Moonstone Publishing, Philadelphia; The Star-Ledger of Newark; NJ Lawyer Magazine; received a NJ Poetry Society 2009 Recognition Award, PoetSpeak on-line and will be published in upcoming volumes of the Edison Literary Review, the Big Hammer, FreeXpresSion, the River Poets Journal, The River and the Blue Collar Review. Four of his poems, have been featured as Poem of the Day by The New Verse News. His poetry was featured on-line in "What's Your Exit? A Literary Detour Through New Jersey."